Under This Roof is a poetry of the [...] everything visible and invisible under the roof of Heaven (which is the way Du Fu and Li Bai thought of it, so why shouldn't you?). The dailiness of family life here mirrors back the momentums of a soul making itself. Most spiritual writing is dominated by the solitude at its heart—what astounds and moves me so much about Monteiro's poetry is the way she takes that solitude, the awareness of suffering and joy in it, and turns it into a shared thing. Though these poems are sometimes bound deeply with loss, there is not a single sour or bitter note to be heard here. In poetry (like life!), thinking needs the breathing space of feeling. Monteiro's work breathes deeply, steadily. It has its wits about it always.

—David Rivard

In Theresa Monteiro's debut *Under This Roof*, one feels like Dante at the outset of his divine journey, as we stand midway along our life's journey, questioning if the right path has been lost. Indeed, these poems come at us from the middle—of a life, of a family, of the choices we have made and are forever bound to as Monteiro tenderly interrogates "the ambiguity of not knowing/if we are headed toward winter or spring." This is a poetry that sifts the sacred from the domestic, that finds grace in the minute yet electric moments of being a mother, wife, and artist. In poems pared down to bone and blood, to muscle and sinew, *Under This Roof* is an extended aria perfectly pitched to sing our grief and ecstasy and the embattled sublimity that is our existence.

—Matt Miller

Theresa Monteiro writes a poetry of movement and open and philosophical consciousness. Full of formal beauty and naturalistic music for us to discover, her poems move through the things of the world the way the best poetry teaches us to see ourselves and the world, grounded in relational love.

—David Blair

Theresa Monteiro's debut *Under This Roof* posits home as both a physical house and a mindset—these are poems of ordinary time that are unabashedly heaven-fixed. Full of wisdom, humility, grief, and hunger, each poem reads as a suburban hymn looking "with one eye open, one eye closed," both inward and outward for the kind of truth that disrupts familiar life. "Were you scrubbing charred/ onions from a pot while/ everything shifted?" the speaker asks, intent on tuning to the miracle at hand. This book is an invitation to see beauty above and beneath familial responsibility—and in doing so, remembering, in the truest sense, the way home.

—Lily Greenberg

Under This Roof

Theresa Monteiro

Under This Roof

Fernwood Press
Newberg, Oregon
www.fernwoodpress.com

Printed in the United States of America

Cover and page design: Mareesa Fawver Moss
Cover art: Kathy Ann Childs
Author photo: Abbie Kiefer

ISBN 978-1-59498-144-9

For Joe

Table of Contents

Some Advice

If a learned man scans
the work of your mind and finds
the meter lacking, unrefined—
put a wolf in your poem.
Because a wolf is not a symbol,
it's a mammal, a carnivore.
Like rusty train wrecks (in which
steel cargo cars lie crumpled
in a field beside aloof cattle) or
someone else's suffering, it's hard
to look away from a wolf. Make him
thin through the hips and thick
around the forelegs and chest.
He is just steps from the shadows
of old conifer trees, bare-trunked
near the ground for having shaded
each other out of flourishing.
There should be a little snow
on the ground, a veneer,
with sharp grasses poking through,
little spears of the earth around his paws.
The ambiguity of not knowing
if we are headed toward winter or spring
keeps the reader's eye moving
from line to line because who can relax
when a wolf (eyes much smaller
than legend would have it, much
closer together on his triangle face,
and more focused than the eyes
of a loyal horse or family dog)
is present? When he turns toward

your reader, make sure it's only
his head that rotates—his body
still oriented toward a grassy valley,
mountains just beyond—
where they meet, invoke
the blue-green color
of a bruise, healing.

I tell you, if they keep silent, the stones will cry out!

—Luke 19:40

Contemplative in the Middle of the World

Stay with me,
silent. Stay, look at me—
I'll look at you, then we'll
stare at the round leaves
of a nameless tree
that shiver like coins,
even with no breeze. Now,
eyes closed,
they're black leaves
in negative space. Through
webs of eyelid-light,
you stand, confident,
at a cliff's edge.
I'm irrationally tall, closer,
your face almost—
a voice in the air. Someone
lost a watch. The cliff,
the leaves, light,
all whir—a window shade
rolled up violently.

In that moment
between cutting the engine
and opening the door,
sit. August sun
heats the steering wheel.
Palms against vinyl feel
a straight burning line,
like a lash

or the dropped stomach
of remembering—
there are different ways
to hear. What you told me
made a sound. The sound
you made was voice and bell
and clean white paper, rustling.

In Plain English

Uncomfortable hearts long
to signify things but not touch
the warm flesh of them.
So, I tell myself solid things:
I have thick ankles,
a few decent poems, and
four dead sons.
These words aren't hard to say
but aren't lyrical, either. Their bodies
came out broken.
Not the sort of trauma one can
elevate with language—
or undo.
If I name them, gossips
turn to whisper. So,
I hide them in hieroglyphs—
cellos, lemons, rivers. For you,
my grief becomes notional. For me,
these gestures are their graves.

Getting an Education

Last night, reading,
I found the word *thistle*,
but I forget the context
because I couldn't, and can't,
call up an image of thistles. I feel
this lack in me—like the
shame of never understanding
imaginary numbers or
what chemists mean
when they talk about a mole.
Ms. Clark was childless, silent,
while this girl asked,
what's a mole? Six point zero two
times ten to the twenty-third power,
of course. An unimaginable number but
not an imaginary number so I try
to imagine a mole of thistles
but can only recall
the down of a thistle which is not
the thistle itself.

I have only learned,
at wakes, to stop myself
from reaching into caskets
to give the bodies reassuring pats,
mumble to them a mole of
motherly things.
The rooms choke on lilies,
carnations, baby's breath,
small purple blooms
like pom-poms—now it comes to me:
You will know them by their fruits.

Greatest Fear of the Mute's Wife

He is carrying a jar
of bread and butter pickles
(a big one from the wholesale club)
in the crook of one arm
and a gallon of milk in the other
to the back-up refrigerator
in the basement. He trips
on a life jacket
some lazy kid or this wife
has thrown down the steps
instead of storing in a bin.
The pickles shatter.
On the cement floor,
unable to cry or call, he waits
for help to find him. Staring up
at duct work and wiring, hearing
water sloshing through pipes
above him—what will he think of?
Maybe, fields arrayed with lilies, how
every bird has its nest,
has its song. Will he remember
every hair on his head
is numbered, though
his voice is gone?
Around his head
milk spreads in patterns
like a crown of lilies
trimmed in blood,
smelling of brine.

New World Symphony

Water over my hands, washing,
of all things, a rolling pin.
I've tried making biscuits.
They'll make me fat, and the kids
happy because they taste like butter
and love. Dvořák plays, a crying oboe,
then a crying child
appears. He's afraid of black holes
because they swallow everything—
rock, paper, scissors.
Here, I say, place your hand
on the speaker, feel the tympany
and vibrations of a lonely violin
just like your own voice
calling after me down a sidewalk
the first time I left you at school.
A ripple of sound I kept
for the day, and until
now. It's like that,
the symphony shaking
our house, above our town,
through blue atmosphere
and black space, bumping
against meteors and comets—
cosmic pinball machine.
Imagine the music
from an immigrant's hand
moving eternally through galaxies
and, maybe, all the way
to a black hole. Can you see
the tiny felt pads of a clarinet, obliterated

by gravity, cellos crushed,
the penciled notes
of a wild-haired conductor
dissolved? But the notes
can't be unmade.
They quiver along the edges
of the vortex, singing:
Going home—
I'm just going home.

Doppler Effect

Rolling of skateboard wheels—
a son leans, carves
a figure eight
through momentum.
Both the approach
and the rolling away—

deafening. Purity of a cricket
song at a distance, hysteria
of a cricket trapped
in the garage. Youth, all blue
waves, compressed,
pressing until pressurized—
it passes. Here

in our millennium of hygiene,
awake on thread-counted sheets,
we hear, *Absalom* in an echo.

Slipping down
from the barber's chair
is a kid who used to be mine.

The Stones Will Cry Out

Behind the student solving proofs
at a kitchen table, a crash
as an ice machine drops cubes
into the freezer's bin.

Accidentally, a toddler pounds
piano keys and plays an
A major chord. All is yellow
and midmorning while

a boy makes a flip-book. Fanning
and fanning its pages—clicks and
tiny breezes in his face.
His animated wheat stalk grows

as colored light rises up
through windows at morning mass
where a going-deaf old woman
prays louder and faster than the others

she cannot hear to match.
Reckless, she drops her kneeler
against the marble. Overhead,

ignorant of its one-pitch
roar, a propeller plane
flies near to earth,
bringing a lover to her love.

So Many Kinds of Hunger

After years of not
crying, she watches
a red cardinal, whose presence
(everyone says) means a loved one,
dead, is near. He rushes
from cherry tree
to windowpane, mornings
all in a row. His flutter-whispers
then violent thwacks
into clean glass
alternate as she considers
lifting the pane and
whooping as a red blur circles
once around the kitchen and
back out to higher branches.

The lyricism comforts until,
taking down cylinders
of black and tan seeds
in bear season, she remembers:
Male grizzlies sometimes
eat their own—
killing their young so
the mamas won't lactate—
be in heat again, soon.

She could knock off stanzas—
birds in flight, lush smells of
spring and saltwater.
But wouldn't it be
insincere? She who
lets the faucet run
while brushing her teeth?

She could use the blood
orange grove and lime trees,
sing of lichen and tadpoles
figuratively—or grizzlies
with blood-matted fur,
digesting their babies,
literally.

Who is This Woman?

She has turned
the fig of antiquity
into a cookie which
nobody likes, made
by a machine of which
the foiled woman
in the salon chair, seen
in a mirror, becomes
a parody—aluminum
in bland precision.
Only in dreaming
does she have her say,
waking so inarticulate,
and so, eventually
silent. Only the robot
woman from the smoke detector
speaks saying, *Fire*
as the toast, or something else,
burns. But she is not
alarmed at all.

Blessed Is the Fruit

Pastel charts in baby books
show proportions:
he was the size of a lemon
when he died.
Lemons. They fit so snugly in the palm,
cool and with a gentle give,
yellow skin so cheerful, dimpled.
Sliced and squeezed, pulp
sticks to fingers—
tart.

Who Knows

A boy with his peanut butter sandwich
        knows nothing
        of the crop crimes committed

in the making of his bread.
        Hunting the pockmarked shore,
        a seagull scavenging

among strips of salted seaweed,
        cigarette butts, and losing
        lotto tickets, knows nothing

of stock market shorts—illusions
        of money, investor reports.
        Some of us, moving apologies

back into tomorrow, unwinding clocks
        and time-crooking days,
        understand poison.

We spread the jelly with the same knife.

Topography of Another April

Associative leaps:
from fear of closed spaces
to the memory of a
bearded bluegrass band
at a sheep-shearing festival.
We don't owe anyone
a map. How did we travel
from the tunnel of a brain scan
to a woman in a tent selling
skeins of woolen yarn
the color of nectarines, varied?

Who wants
the closed loop of a story
that ends, neatly?
But it's enough to say
the youngest was two.
He watched the fiddle, unable
to look away, bouncing
his bottom to a song
singing of life in a time
before sarcoma clinics—
when eight-gauge needles came
in pairs of carved bamboo.
The pattern repeats:
knit one, purl two.

Bread and Circus

My son, twelve, worries
ammo from an AK-47 shot
from our front lawn could blast
through all the walls of our house:
siding, sheathing, insulation, drywall.
One would pierce a sepia photo
of Nona, leaning over a lapful
of pea pods, snapping off
stems, tossing them back
into the skirt of her dress.
One would blast a hole
in the eye of a wallpaper-swallow
on a field of beige
behind Nona. Into the belly
of the upright piano, shells would
snap taught strings, hammers would
splinter and whelp. The glass frame
of a Pisarro print we hung
above our mantle could shatter.
And what if one reaches
the backyard—what if it lodges
(at rest now) in the chest of someone,
eyes closed, head tilted
against the back of a blue
Adirondack chair?
It would happen so fast
he couldn't decide to die,
singing.

Solomon Says

Wisdom is more mobile than any motion.
Where does she go? Can't she be
still? She's a mother
who will never say, *First this,*
then that. Simultaneity
always because her wound
is not her own and all work
revolves. Mama's gotta
fry an egg while she spells
cantaloupe, c-a-n-t—she can't
have an arse ache unless
you have one too. Looped
over the forefinger: a key ring.
Over the middle finger: grocery bag
of shallots and bananas. Now
she's twilight singing, varying
the rhythm as she holds:

aging bodies
acorns
medicinal smells
memories
of sutures
a wallet-sized photograph
signed in ballpoint ink
time (un-chronological)
bright coupons
the same broken whistle

All of this she carries
on her hip—light, undivided.

Prayer for a Life Longer Than a Sonnet

You tell me, persevere my little duck.
You tell me, turn the wheel my faithful mule.
But look at all the cornflakes in my car—
like Sisyphus I vacuum and they're back
again. I try to match up all the socks.
I'm tired.
See the puffy purple eyes, like mine,
of this bent woman at the park? She's sure
everything I need is in her purse.
No thanks. Keep your know-it-all mean spirits,
your lectures on my wallet, and your pills.

Sometimes, I would like us to live the life
of scallops clustered at the bottom
of a shallow sea, visited by planks
of geometric light—and Lord,
let me die like a scallop.
The starfish pull is slow, invading,
prying open my shell to eat my insides,
a briny lunch. A drawn-out death, yes,
but it will take me that long to be ready
to say goodbye.

Wild

Wildebeests cross
a brown river of crocodiles.
The herd's too big to turn—

they plunge wildly forward.
Some are eaten, some make it
to plains of good grass,

grateful. For the wildebeest,
home is the side of the river
where it's alive, where it is fed.

For us, wild is neither *home* nor
not home. Wild is searching—
always moving. In grief

I pray, get me home. Plant me
in new ground. I cannot walk
old ground today.

I am wild. I'm growing
like a stalk of bloodroot
in a parking lot, sprouting

from pavement cracks,
green shoot splitting open
painted white lines. Free me—

from concrete weight, from
calendar pages of dates
when someone died and left

shoes and envelopes or nothing.
A clutter of memories (office chairs,
photographs taped to the wall) fall off

like the white petals of the bloodroot,
so slender they never touch until
they shrivel together on the ground.

Does the flower let go of the petal
or the other way 'round? I let go
of eyes and names and lose my way.

The face of the baby is gone. A child
is coming. He's a toddler, wild
and drawn to a staircase

as the avocado rushes to brown—
my God, how to remember the way
home? I remember the sound

of purple phlox sprouting wild
with honeybees, the color of
common milkweed, and the

smell of grandmothers while
the bloodroot with its yellow stamen
wilts and dies where it grew.

But it makes the ground new.
And I can live on this ground,
for now. I plant my grief here

with boneset and salvia and
plump bees drink all that nectar
and sorrow. Having traveled

far and growing tired
of sentiment, I will
sit in the grass and wait.

The Prelude to Bach's First Solo Cello Suite

rises and rises
making the sound of people
being good—or at least trying. It dips
the way they fail then
climbs again. Bats and small birds
who cannot fly the altitudes
duck and soar a bit.
The rising, like a drug,
reminds us of good people.
Called, good people walk
into need. She needed to know,
that woman unaccustomed to children,
why the baby, newly walking,
didn't cry. Over and over
he fell, rose bottom first, hands
to the ground, laughing, stepping,
falling. I didn't have an answer
for her then, or now, except—
he was not alone—no more than
the solo cello is—
it only seems alone. Notes
ascend in patterns while
a deep blue chord, soul of some
invisible instrument, lifts the climber
from beneath. Only four strings? Impossible—
but there it is. The vibrato
of autumn coming, dark
before dinner, cold
every morning—Canada geese
stop chasing park-goers for crumbs
and form majestic Vs.

The pleasure in the dark is knowing
how glorious the light will be.
Listening to the geese above
the cello playing above the other
invisible cello, I remember
how good it is to eat bread—
and we can still eat bread at a table.
I can still walk to get from one place to
the loud river. It is good to write,
lying on the floor with
one eye open, one eye closed.

The Speed of Light

We can't say *Truth*, now. We can't
make singular, or *one*, what is
privatized. But isn't light,
in the distance, on a fog-thick night
where damp makes cold
colder, *real*? In the distance,
the colored light
of a gray house fills out
four over four glass panels and
to the smoker and the dog walker
is agreeable. Truth: We agree

about the speed of light because
it has a number value.
To travel at that rate
would bring a girl out from,
and back to, Earth, younger
than her classmates left behind,
they, aged and gawking, deciding
whether to envy or pity this child
who cannot go back to childhood. Here,
she finds drones and phones
beaming blue light across the spectrum
of believed things. She would like to

go back to an old glow. She remembers
the table lamps in her living room
as a child (in body and time).
The lamps flanked the sofa
beneath the deep bay window.
If she couldn't get a seat
beside her mother while she read aloud

she would climb inside the windowsill
and look over Mama's head, down
to the sketchy illustrations of
giant people and peaches. But

it's the light she wants to hold again,
from the lamps. She'd tap the warm pad
of any fingertip to the brassy body of the lamp and
the bulb glowed, a little. A second tap made things
brighter and one more touch would set
the whole room burning—
whichever child in the windowsill
made present to whomever
(a smoker or a dog walker)
passed in the night. She wants to know, now,
how the skin told the lamp told the bulb
to pace itself.

Truth has sometimes
come to me this way,
not moving at its own speed,
but mine. First, at a slant.
Then, face first. Then,
crushing, lovely, reflected,
not traveling anywhere,
at any speed,
just holding.

How else would God speak to me, if not through my imagination?

—St. Joan of Arc

Under This Roof

1.

On earth, a roof
of solar rectangles turns
east to west. A corner shingle,
close to a spruce, collects
a thickness of sap
and bird droppings. It absorbs
nothing, contributes
nothing. Under this roof,
recessed lights flicker above
a table where a couple eats
their shadowy veal.

I'm sorry, she says. Which is
not enough and also
so very much. Simultaneously,
the sharp sound of forks against plates
and the thrumming of a moderate rain
picking up.

2.

Poets claim a broken heart—
as if a heart were still there,
left of the sternum
just fragmented—beating
sorrow. One poet tries
to make its sound:
A shopping cart's broken wheel
faltering left in whiny iambs.
Some woman slouches, pushes,
doesn't choose another cart.

Maybe this poet means
a poisoned heart?
Something strange between the lungs,
communicator of murky
blood inside a woman, in a basement,
flooding. The woman watches it fill.
There, a seasonal wreath
all silk flowers and plastic petals floats
above the floor. Hypnotized
by yellow water pooling
around her feet, she knows her
shoes will shrink—
and this, reader (you understand)
is not about the shoes.

But no—not a parenthetical!
You understand—
part of the whole,
at least.

3.

Bent over stacks of paper,
candlelight reflected
off their tonsures,
monks thread pages
of *summas*, silent.
Aquinas sighs—
This work is straw.

Past late winter pastures
of grasses dormant below earth
buried in frost,

in a stable, a heavy cow
shelters her calf against
her milky belly, lowing
on a bed of straw—
warm while waiting
for the thaw and light.

Give us that word, like the thread
pulled through, binding the pages,
cut off from the spool
at the proper time
with the teeth.
A word that is enough.

4.

Ask Alighieri: Purgatory is full
of art—word made image.
On one hand, walls of beauty,
on the other,
scenes of regret.
In a lesser poem,
it's a mother,
licking her thumb,
washing the foreheads
of ordinary souls
slower than needed; she scrubs
each child clean, holding
each chin in her hand
for a moment. She says: *Behold, now*
you'll understand the whole.
She sends them on their way

where they find no paralegals
among the Church Triumphant.
They've left pencils and
neckties on the ground. Traded them
for singing—the off-key, with each
word, matching pitch.

5.

Some scholars think
it's wrong to say *Behold!*
in poems now. It doesn't
sound like speech.

But—behold, the moon!
Don't just look—
hold your gaze, see?
We know it's a sphere
but appears to us
a flat disc. Perfect white
circumference carved
in the tarmac of the sky admitting
glow from a source behind.

Behold flesh
thin as the skin
of an inner wrist
held against vestments
of a martyr's feast day.
See brightness of arterial blood—
seventy times seven threads
through the eye of the needle
opened wide.

We have only begun
to imagine the fullness of life.
How could we tire of hope?
—so much is in bud.

—Denise Levertov

In the Beginning

Computers break down old mythologies
of forces and vital fluids

into step-by-step depictions
of the moment cells collide—the cells

mix their essences,
fill out the pairs, divide, multiply.

Understanding sees atoms
link, proteins form,

lipids hydrophobically
turn in on themselves.

Then, since each cell knows
its role, a heart beats;

a rounded bottom forms,
and folded arms, fingernails, eyelids.

An intake of breath, an exhale, and
a new cry vibrates filtered air.

But slowing down the process
tells us nothing we want to know.

A boy looks up from his cereal bowl,
milk drips from his chin, spoon frozen halfway.

He asks: *Why don't turtles love their babies?*

William and the Fox

From the den, where spines of
linen books shine from wear, and piles
of drafts live on tables by a record player,

crackling and skipping, he watches
a fox. From her neat teeth
dangles a limp mouse.

He would like to believe that
the fox and the mouse are one—
circle of life and all—

that the rain needs our pity and
our submission. As the buffalo nods
to the grass, he nods. Tomorrow he will

garden with the tenderness of
the pink tulip petals.
But today he hears, *love*

and writes an image
of anisette cookies lined up
in straight rows, lit up

by sugar and color,
behind curved glass.
Then, from above, comes

one cookie announcing itself
with the sound of waxed paper.
Behind the paper hovers

the pinched brim of a wool cap.
And everything smells like his father.
And he cannot forgive the fox.

From Inside the Whirlwind

A blow to the head, she collapsed
on the bed, waking
to find the wind blowing
fear and chickens in circles
by her window—but those
and the yellow brick road were all
in her mind. Sadness lingers
recalling the warm colors
of poppies, acres of orange
and red blooms. Even the sleep
was in her sleep. Now, see

how today spins? *I am Dorothy,*
her house pulled up
in a cyclone of dream.
Everything passing is mournful—
a subway station, a county fair,
a familiar room—and every passing
image passes again—gray messenger
bag of bills, a corndog or catalog.
Each a symbol of any Tuesday's

suffering. But how to acquire the habit
of seeing the thing itself?
Wrapped in greasy paper,
the corndog is smaller, the little girl
eating it, unashamed.
With spokes of red, yellow,
orange, white, the Ferris wheel
stands perpendicular to the sea.

Still, I choose
the inner space of the mind,
every time. I say: The world
grieves and outer space is
desolate. You say: But look
at the view from a shuttle! Look
at the glass-blue marble of the world
floating. Go there. Feel
the creak of a stair underfoot.
Or watch, with a child's
small joy, as the ring around
the number four lights up
when you press it—
feel the elevator
loft you up,
holding all your weight.

Suburban Hymn

Stuck in my craw:
To say, *I praise you*, is not
to praise. It rattles
hollow—one penny in a tin-can bank.
The can in an empty room sounds
its echoing clang, the clang
diminishing, the way
a cry for help falls deeper
into canyons in cowboy movies—
half-life of sound, shrinking.
But the sound
of flattery (which has volume)
is not praise. Praise the world
by making lists?
-A veiny hand along a banister in half-light
-A honeybee landing on a curved branch of catmint, bobbing
-Clean fire on a cold night
No.
Say praise and mean,
tell the truth.
Say praise but mean,
I don't deserve what's here.
What's here is the penny—
its small, raised face
so serious and precise.
Who decided the least worthy
coin should be the loveliest color?
Who invented the tin-can bank,
soft beans swapped for
copper-joy of little worth?

It rattles, not hollow, but makes
a solid sound like a pang (of hunger, regret)
and a baby laughs at the sound,
a deep, flowering laugh, growing
louder as it spreads. She laughs
at the penny sound, at how
silly all the small things are.

To Tell You the Truth

It's easy to sympathize with the glacier, now,
and its melting. Anyone can see
the polar bear's strife, can hear
the honeybee's muted buzz. But I know
dear Magellan, my medieval self with
her children buried by some
plague would have leered
in the crowd—thrown an onion,
rotten, at your face. How could I
see the stars above, their promise,
and believe they burned below me, too?
Oh, the dream of falling off the edge
of creation into some strangeness—
less horrible than a lifetime
of traveling in a straight line only
to end up in the same place.

Who Sees

Praying mantis of the
        high voltage power lines
        keep their hours

above the traffic circle.
        Each car enters, surrenders
        to centrifugal force, is launched

toward a diner, a liquor store,
        home. At home
        left hands see all

the business of the rights:
        mylar balloons, soup cans, penciled letters
        printed just below

the dotted line. Below the power lines
        only two squirrels
        see the mail carrier step

over a sidewalk chalk drawing.
        He drives his mother to the salon
        every Friday.

Third Decade

The fruit of the mystery is
courage. But even iron,
holding the world together,
would prefer to rust,
to break down. He wants
to be *seen*—
but here I am,
making a casserole like
it's all I know. Be courageous
like peaches in winter—
like black frog eggs holding
heat till spring. Be courageous.
Ask the question you know
will make him cry, then,
don't leave.
A sometimes oracular truth:
What we need comes after
the first moment in which we need it.

Road Trip

The argument always amounts to
humility: Who gets
to be the giver?
Who must receive?
Say nothing, look
out the window.

Plywood resting
against a tire pile reads
*Maple Syrup and Campwood
Here*—our differences on display:
you blow on embers forever,
I need reckless blaze—
I feed it everything, live
at the boiling point.

White River, color of jade stone,
pushes to our right, discursive—
messy with what the beavers
left behind. Like children (like us)
beavers craft with destruction.
By some sleight of hand
the river's on our left now.
How did we miss
traveling over it?
How did our speech
slip beneath us?

At an echoing church,
we pray—our *Hallelujahs* rise
cascade back down,
but louder. What's left
of the sun divides
though colored window shapes.
It's clear.

Twins

A pulsing in the womb—thump,
shush-shush. Smaller than a teacup,
lighter than a tulip,
flutter of toes. Can I tell
how a soul, inside a body, within a body
feels? A foot beneath my ribs.

But two twisting and rolling
in the waters? I count
their movements every hour.
How can you tell
which is moving?
The same way I can tell
your hand from mine
when we hold them.

Born, swaddled, capped—
nurses split brother and sister
into glass bassinets.
Without his head cradled
in the crook of her neck, he cries.
Two in the morning,
a pillowed lap, a child at each breast,
hungry swallowing the only sound
in the comatose night.

German friends—where is your
twelve-letter word to tell of
my unworthiness? I cannot name it.

Linguistics

That twist-pluck of peach from stem
when it's August-ripe is the easy
wrist-flick of a promise made.
I promise: some kids will thrive,
swim the blue ocean, play
the French horn, and some will live
to be old. *Like the boy with curly hair,*
she asks, *who is the same temperature
of a cheetah?* Yes, and we hold
the china cups we've left unsaid.
We want no love made bitter
by bad translation—that taste
left on fingers from counting pennies
all day only to find what looked like treasure
won't buy much. This love (and others
the same speed as trees) makes
the sound of sense. The way bread
is the touch of old wallpaper in a house
where we are safe, full of chocolate
making the sound of sleep.
Her fingers twist around mine.
I can promise a few things as sharp
as all the sharp parts of crocodiles.

For Luke On Your Fourteenth Birthday

But the hanging lamps
are slices of octagon!
Filaments line their insides,
so, looking up, I think of
honeycomb between me and heaven.

How strange! So many years
in the same pew, never noticing.
Now, the light thickens too—

as if, entering a familiar
room where someone has changed
the bulbs, inserted more efficient ones,
more natural than the old glow,
the space (once, as invisible as home)
is altered, sweetly uncomfortable.

Everyone has those dreams.
You return to your childhood home.
Every bit of kitsch and each chair
as it was—except
behind doors appear rooms
you never knew existed:

ballrooms, libraries, extra kitchens,
a gymnasium maybe—each
a place for possibility. But how
(you will ask yourself in the dream)
did you not know?
Were you scrubbing charred
onions from a pot while
everything shifted?

On Martyrdom

Nice is not a virtue, he says.
Everyone's buying chocolates
on account of Valentine who was
beheaded for love. He says,
Anyone can be sweet
for a price. I ask:
What about the brutal February
of your life? What about loneliness
and doubt, forgetting to
look into mirrors and say:
Yes, I am dull, shrinking,
and still love. Because, what
(since we have only one word
for it) you look and find a love
of comfort—or worse, a love
of admiration? What if you have no
burned-at-the stake kind of love? What if
you fall asleep reading Hass and dream
you're reading Hass? The words on the page end
and the white page disappears
somewhere to your left, and of course
the poems aren't his. Maybe they're yours
but you won't remember them
when you wake. You wake remembering
you have memorized almost nothing—
you write poems on recycled paper.
You touch the triangle of arrows and understand
the paper used to have different words (in its last life)
words like *lamb chops* and *Palmolive*,
outlined in black dashes to show women
where to cut, how to save.

American cheese is so much a pound—
with the coupon, so much less.
The cheese is dyed yellow,
just like your paper was
before it was poetry, but after
it was a tree dropping its leaves for us
to rake up and squash into paper bags and he says,
Raking's not a virtue either, it's just control.
Blow the leaves into the woods
and do something hard. Which is easy
to say, until you look in the mirror,
smiling, and find you are
the mother opossum, all ten babies
hanging from your fur—you're foraging
and find the pit of an apricot with flesh
still clinging.

The Process of Revision

The poem made it clear: I grieved.
But how to say *I'm still battered*?
Because the dead are dead
each morning, every day
calls for all the business
of being still alive.
Like a mutt swept up
into a river in flood I keep
my head above water
without knowing why.

Revise: Use another dog—
that three-legged dog from my past.
Still, with a hind leg gone
he was fast! When another was lost
he bounced on his two front feet.
For three months,
beside the red house,
kids kissed his happy face.
He chased them in his wobbly handstand.

Grief alters: Change
the image of the dog
to a goat, unblinking, climbing,
up and down a rocky ledge,
aimless to the onlooker.
Revise: The goat is a mother goat,
the ledge is a barnyard, and her kid
butts everything. In a month,
maybe, the goats will be
donkeys—plowing, resigned.
Furrowing furrows in parallel rows,
they know the fruits are not their own.

But where is that dog? In a draft
on the floor, torn in half
by my shame: grief shouldn't
look like that. But shame lies
about the value of everything—
relentless.

Upstream

He is sleeping. I can't tell
him: We will never again
sit in boats—not him, anyway.
Pila said, in the next world,
he will tell me a joke
in his own voice
again. I believe her.
But will there be boats?
I'm asking: Will there be any
need for an orange kayak
like the one we paddled down
that warm river, in pink light,
our guide calling it a river
without snakes, without
death—too calm for drowning?
What did he know? What
did we know about
all the ways to die? Did we believe
in death? We do now.
And when it comes, are there roads
to walk, or rivers? It will be all joy
I'm sure, but asking:
Though we might be able to fly,
give us a kayak of any color,
a snakeless river,
and though no time exists,
one afternoon.

Hope of Holy Week

Round-bellied priest
crosses the parking lot
with a coffee cup, limping.

Smell of incense, a bell,
a man singing out of time, loudly.
The collection basket floats.

Unleavened hosts bought
from the internet, still
unbloodied, still.

***

One locust lands
on the back of her hand
beside a blister from the grinding stone.

Dried fish, salted
hang from a string. Pearly eyes—
a desert breeze ripples the scales.

Sour figs, slashed, sweetening
at midnight. Somewhere
someone is awake and hungry.

***

The magnolia blooms
white—fragile blossoms
without leaves.

Below two skies in two hours,
mourning doves find a twist tie
from a plastic bread bag.

They weave it with dandelion stems
for a nest. When has your despair
predicted anything true?

Safe Harbor

A place he only saw once
gave him hope—there was open ocean
crashing and vertical, without
mansions on cliffs—just shoreline
and a few modest lobster boats
putting out early into the morning
and into whatever was past where he could see.
And how much verse has he found
about this wildness? The waves
or the exact shade of blue at noon? But here,
I want to tell you about nothing
and silence.
Not absence of noise but openness
to everything, how his skin felt
heat from the rock beneath while
his eyes followed a skimming cormorant.
Then, like a ghost, Frost whispered,
suggesting we all second guess
ourselves with his *far and deep*—
but what if farther and deeper
are kinds of greed? What if
neither direction matters, just stillness?
Stillness which my father needed
to watch the lobster boat shrink.
Still, in order to see a black seal's head,
then gone. But now, to go home
to a place of commerce and parking spots
freshly painted the same size or
slightly smaller than his car and where
the checkout lines are numbered. So,
he hangs a wind chime, blunt and square

from the crossbeam of his porch—a wind chime
meant to mimic buoys in that bay.
There's the neighbor, walking
her poodle, unrolling a neat green bag
to clean up little Ginger's mess while
her husband taps golf balls into a cup
on the front lawn, always moving
in inches. But none of this is sad—
not the little bag or the clipped grass
ornamented with pinwheels and small flags.
Because my father knows the difference
between the rocky shoreline
and the view from his porch, is nothing
compared with the distance between that ocean
and the stillness that's to come.

Acknowledgments

Thank you to these publications in which versions of these poems first appeared:

Cutleaf Literary Journal "Some Advice," "Suburban Hymn"
Rumblefish Quarterly "Contemplative in the Middle of the World"
Tipton Poetry Journal "Getting an Education"
The American Journal of Poetry "Greatest Fear of the Mute's Wife"
The Meadow "New World Symphony"
Pittsburgh Poetry Journal "Who Is This Woman?"
Black Fork Review "Blessed Is the Fruit"
Presence: A Journal of Catholic Poetry "Prayer for a Life Longer
     Than a Sonnet"
The Banyan Review "The Prelude to Bach's First Solo Cello Suite"
On the Seawall "The Speed of Light," "William and the Fox"
Dunes Review "On Martyrdom"
River Heron Review "Safe Harbor"

Title Index

First Line Index